KING ATTERBERRY INK

JOEL WASHINGTON ATTERBERRY

IN LOVING MEMORY
OF MY GRANDMOTHER
GEDELL HICKSON-FELDER HARRIS

THE BEAUTIFUL WOMAN WHO
RAISED ME!

King Atterberry Ink

Copyrighted © 2021 Library of Congress.

Published by: Joel Washington Atterberry

ISBN: 978-1735295237

Contact Information

Email: kingatterberry7@gmail.com

Facebook: Joel Washington Atterberry

Instagram: king_atterberry7

Instagram: king_atterberry_ink

Editor: Julia C. Dozier

Illustration Cover: Christine Jones

Illustration Graffiti: Robert Ross aka Logan

My Atterberry Way!

I can only be me and will not change for anybody.

Accepting who I am, and not compromising my own character to make another person's insecurities strengthen off my shoulders will never happen.

JWA is a friend of a friend till the end.

Every day is a fight to stay walking on the path even if you must change routes.

It is about staying in tune with the Most High.

Living beyond the narrative of expectation!

Author Biography

One of Harlem's own, born, bred and raised on the West Side of town.

With a keen eye, I absorbed everything that Harlem was. Socially, culturally, artistically; including everything from the characters that paraded these blocks before, presently, and after me. From their hustling spirit for survival, to the style of fashion these denizens projected as they navigated the concrete jungle.

I took my talents across the water to the Garden State, and that has been home for a few decades. The funny thing about NYC is that when you're there you don't realize just how fast time and life is moving around you until you leave.

My departure from the city helped me cultivate perspective and hone my writing skills, and although I occasionally travel the city from time to time, in essence I've brought the city with me everywhere I go...the memories, the scents, the focus, and the flair for life that Harlem instills in a person.

The late great Bobby Womack once famously sang "Harlem is the capitol of every ghetto town." I hold these truths to be self-evident. To say these Harlem streets shaped me is an understatement and for that I'm thankful and grateful.

Inspired by the spirit of the great Langston Hughes, Ralph Ellison, Zora Neale Hurston, Paul Robeson, Duke Ellington, and Sammy Davis Jr, how could I not tap into my inner potential and manifest something great when those same creatives walked in the same streets before me.

Currently residing in South Jersey, Cape May County, has afforded me the gift of reflection away from the hustle and bustle of the city and I am grateful to be able to put my thoughts, feelings, emotions, and experiences in poet fashion.

Here I found my true calling, working in healthcare assisting and connecting with others. Gleaning onto the words and wisdom of people who have lived their lives and contemplate their mortality with each advancing breath.

In my 21-year experience in the field something happened over the last 6 years in which experiences were in desperate need to be documented. No longer could I internalize life, so I started documenting and renewing my creative spirit in the form of poetry, songs and living parables.

In other words, "I've been getting busy!" Eleven poetry books later and far from finished, I'm still going and for that I would like to thank my ancestors, my family and my supporting cast that fuel the fire in me. Our virtual poetry show is doing very well, and so is my writing, through the divine clearance of thought. It's been one helluva rise on the ride while elevating around newer people.

So, I ask for you to journey through these pages and see a walk-through of my life experiences.

Thank you!

Acknowledgements

Special appreciation to my son:
JOEL J.

Peace and love to my brothers:
Prescott and Hassan.

Peace and love to my sister Jawhara.

Peace and love to my uncles:
Lester, Darren, Destin, Anton, and Branden.

Peace and love to my Aunts:
Janice, Patricia, Gloria, Sandra, Shea,
and Tammy.

Peace and love to my Cousins:
THEO CEASAR & Vicki Val
You already know.

Peace and love to Andre and Renea Ravenell.
I cannot thank you both enough.
You already know.

Peace and love to Terri, Kammy, and Estelle.

Peace and love to Julia C. Dozier for always
giving me an alley-oop with my projects and
being a great friend.

Peace and love to Tisha Bowen
for always being more like a sibling than a
cousin to me, and lil jazzy your daughter for
looking up to me like an uncle and a cousin,
and to Aunt Pat for helping me when I was
younger!

Peace and love to Cousin Sarah Hickson who
took on the role in my life as an aunt.

Peace and love to Jimmie Brown aka Mommy
and family for having my back when I needed
you.

Peace and love to my Atterberry, Wiggins
and Dowling families.
All of you gave me some thoughts to
manifest on within life.

"GRATITUDE"

Peace and love to my Cousin,
Rob-Logan who always comes through on
time.

Peace and love to the Ross brothers.

Peace and love to Celina, Nicole, and Charles
Johnson.

Table of Contents

MINDFUL THOUGHTS

It's what I do.

Before my prime I started caring about the
written lines.
Placing words together as some women
opened up my mind.
Many poets I heard before that I was able to
understand.
But I knew one day I would comprehend and
be a real fan.
As a young dude became influenced by all
these others that were writers.
Sensational divers creative night spot flyers.
Smooth with the flow of placing emotions on
paper.
Learned to give it all I got turned doubters
into waiters.
Some of the ladies were pleased with my
material to read.
The more paper they received the more my
craft started to reach.
In person my freestyle made it hard for some
to breathe.

That hypnotic super sonic sensual topics had them hug and squeeze.
The cool cat with the poetry raps wore my cap to the back.
My fascination for this genre made me cool like dat.
Muses providing ideas and concepts with me writing on the fly.
I will always be in love with poetry until I die!

King Atterberry Ink

Move across margins left and right
mentality.
My reality is challenged by this off world
tragedies.
Rich in heart illuminate in dark without an
angel seen.
My new rhyme scheme shows a picture with
my new meme.
This is what I do is logo in this poet's
hand.
I'm powered by father's father spirit, you
don't understand.
Same initials issued by a judge it is all
legal now.
Gentlemen quality style feel my verse I'm
never out bounds.
In my bag ancestral jewelry on whichever
wrist.
My off days of working I am smoking
California cannabis.
Mixed drink on deck as I pen pad new
material.

Got that justice league aura that is how I
become lyrical.

Ride waves of my poetry, colleagues and
members.

The 'Poetry Corner' book was manifested
just remember.

Join elites not to compete but give a treat
that run deep.

As I reach many mountains and stall tall on
grounded peaks.

Hansolo

Mental mind master maneuvering moving mountains.

Forever flipping fresh fascinations finding fountains.

Cool courageous cats climbing center circles colossal.

Hurry helps holistically healing health how honorable.

Deep divine devotion demonstrating dope dynamics.

Application apparently applied around astonished.

People picture public problems persuaded pleasing peace.

Lost leaders looking losing life lie living leaked.

Barricade benefits behavior beyond blast bastards.

Pen stroke

Delicate and deadly expressing words chosen.
Hypnotic line posting centered around motion.
Avalanched thoughts sent through the blood vessel.
Ignite the wrist to move fingers writing something special.
Bless the ears that hear not for cheers and flare.
Formulating ideas from nowhere when it appear.
Sharp as stencils on point like pencils Spark the mental.
Mystic mind essential my potential is residential.
It's home sweet home in and out of my comfort zone.
Vibrating within the tone giving sounds of a xylophone.
Emerge from my inner self aura high on the glow.
It's the mode that unfold when it's exposed key the code.
Is it in the air that you breathe as you manifest your dreams.
Perhaps the natural drug injected to perform a rhyme scheme.
My scene come alive after my drive of motivation.
Providing flows with lines my cadence is on vacation

Beautiful beverage

No biracial coffee strictly mild roasted lattes.
You already carry Splenda in your center
may I venture.
To a journey of an amazing exploration visit
your galaxy.
Speak to your universe through time and
space i would gladly.
Open the door to my partially closed inner
connectivity.
Travel through vicinities and leave you lovely
memories.
When I see them pretty eyes with the style of
your smile.
I would love an invitation with a when, why
and how.
My oneness with the air to find your prayers
anywhere.
May my gesture appear and be fair lend me
your ear.
To speak words into existence I am vigilant
upon meeting you.

Yes, I am pursuing someone I find special guess who.

Old soul of a man who stays youthful in his heart.

Allow me to start this great adventure with a spark.

Kiss your thoughts with the passion of a starry evening.

This is full moon affection I hope that you believe in.

True strength of sight beyond lights that illuminate.

Look at my face as I demonstrate expression yes, I can wait.

Beige boy breathing

Working a job, it's a job within a job of a job.
Soon as your day start, pick up a card and
get charged.
Never will these devils get another chance to
move.
Throw some salt on their wound as they
body consume.
Whichever is the preference that have life
twisted.
I get it, yet remember who you mixing with.
When I join leagues it's to proceed on my
belief.
Never do I lose sleep on days becoming free.
Biggest treat is a time to rock with those that
is nice.
Take percentage off the price and roll the hot
dice.
Numbers looking shaky nerves achy off the
pot.
Throw time off my watch as I dip from any
spot.

My play never theatrical see the live feed anytime.

I keep quarters for arcadians even snitches keep dimes.

My line of women type is involved with gods might.

Fright will never bite or ignite a war to fight.

Hold on, I view the strong that is warm that I would arm.

Give a look with my eyes present a smile with charm.

It is the guardian king atterberry forever ready.

Rock steady and end February with some confetti.

Must be the season pt.2

Good afternoon to the world I'm out the door
headed to work.
Physical full of morning vibes feet stepping
on dirt.
Gotta make the bus time is moving across
my wristwatch.
Can't be late clocking in penalty time your
docked.
Thinking as if I manifested Star Trek doctor
Spock.
Common sense on lock so I made it filling a
slot.
My read-on personalities of the building that
I'm in.
Is a fifty-fifty got damn energy wasted again.
So, I pretend to bend the laws of nature and
book a galaxy.
Exit a timeline enter a universal fantasy.
Destiny is calling me should I dip out and dip
back.
Nah I been there with that crap keep my
peace hat.

Always born on the norm until you witness
me gone.

What remain is a song or a poem not written
long.

Just through my expression what I adapt to I
have to.

I'm a king rich at heart with no crown, throne
or castle.

Moving around with believers, achievers and
peacekeepers.

Beware of those that cheat us fronting like
they please us.

Double standard on the lookout we saw it
before it came.

Must be the season pt.2 JWA is the name.

It's only right

Teamed up with negotiators and left alone
debaters.
Had a talk with the creator and asked for
gods' favor.
Changed up my flavor and spoke to different
neighbors.
Service the area with potential multiplies my
wages.
Cases increasing, we the know the reason
it's the season.
Complicated breathing have me changing
how I'm eating.
Single no cheating I don't knock the ones
creeping.
Wake up from sleeping enjoy a nice, beautiful
weekend.
Hit my spots so the balance of life remains
steady.
May as well get ready to hear some old
school medleys.
Push my vehicle up the parkway then hit the
turnpike.

Headed to north Jersey and New York so I can get right.

There's a opportunity in both vicinities I'm involved with.

Position held hostage waiting for me to start quick.

Release what's held dearly to me see it come back.

No battle on my dreams it's all love no combat.

Chorus:

It's only right to sleep tight when it's almost midnight.

Lamp off only light is the tv on my eyesight.

Dim Setting, memory of the day gone I'm resting.

When I wake up do my prayers, so my spirit feel the blessings.

Play your position!

Next day apply for a seat next to the greatest.
Don't have to be a favorite too much hype get
wasted.
Grab a hold of some wonderful experience.
Skill set amazing nothing flagrant period.
Serious method when I begin writing on my
down time.
Lines never hard to find making designs.
Climb up blocks of buildings covering many
ceilings.
America needs healing watchtowers need
feelings.
Therefore, hope is found turned around
through our sound.
Poetry power pumped up hitting those other
grounds.
Speak what you know not about the blurry
visions.
Beyond the truth what's missing is how
some don't listen.
What's the cost to pay attention without a
hateful living?

Why keep forgetting and switching speaking with tension.

My mission is bringing a community out of friction.

Time to make a change and play your right position.

FEBRUARY FOR US

Like Countee Cullen my work speaks for
itself throughout its own rights.
My Nat turner intuition allows my spirit to
stand tall and fight.
This edition is nothing new just something
freshly brewed.
May not have walked in our heroes' shoes
but I damn near came close to.
Getting myself in trouble for being
opinionated like Muhammad Ali.
I refuse to live and breathe off the lies that
are spoken to me.
Capture the essence and presence of my
imagery like Aaron Douglass.
Play with sounds like Louis
Armstrong, Garvey's movement still amongst
us.
Extend my hand like Claude McKay with my
James Weldon Johnson display.
My piece is covered by the spirit of Malcolm
X and Langston Hughes' ways.

Same way Harriett moved through cape may,
Nj around 1852.

In 1700 Richard Allen made things happen in
Philly without a clue.

As a youth I was Inspired by Walter dean
Myers with a Claude brown attitude.

My personal views lift the troops and alley
hoop them with gratitude.

My people

1821 dry scouring was invented by Thomas
Jennings.

Sarah Boone in 1892 the iron board was a
beginning.

Pants and shirts pressed up or taken to the
cleaners.

One hell of a job created by some of our
dreamers.

Thanks to Benjamin Banneker the first,
building a clock.

George Washington carver scientific with
peanut crops.

The hand pencil sharpener was created by
john L love.

In 71 cell phones created by henry t
Sampson.

Double inventor Garrett Morgan gas mask
and traffic light.

Both can save life in between sight and
breathe on sites.

Marie van Brittan brown gave us the first
home security.

Not many homes had them only rich ones
plus facilities.
James e west created the electronic
microphone.
3D glasses created by Kenneth Dunkley we
saw the zone.

A Woman's Worth

As a man who recognize the internal voice
that speak.
As a man treat your lady with respect by
showing humility.
Keep her covered inside the belt of love and
be considerate.
My sisters don't live in the moment with
those idiots.
Be who you were meant to be a breath of
fresh air.
Absorb the true nature of another who
genuinely care.
Build a will that's strong enough to handle
whirlwinds.
Receive noted attention without having to
mention.
Queen with high self-esteem live out your
dreams.
Walking and talking inside of a world that's
un-clean.
Your passion is seen and fueled by lucky
charms.

Fly through a storm that might be born
outside of the norm.
Only you can determine what is and what it is
not.
If a full moon can make the earth unbalanced
ground your spot.
As I allow this piece to drop without the
picture getting cropped.
I give you women props fighting against what
is a lot.

ELABORATE FORCE FIELD

Live and direct

Stand close enough to kings and feel that hope is alive.

It's hard to lean on faith when your spirit ain't high.

Gotta bring our whole soul to a place where its good.

Find yourself a nice look and indulge in open books.

Given to the ones it's the words that free concern.

Exercise the mind to find time while earn and learn.

Shift outside yourself whatever's felt can resurrect.

That feeling you thought left came back control your breath.

Science of understanding is moving all that block.

Perhaps if clocks stop take advantage of what you spot.

Seize all moments available while the tide change.

Close your eyes and realize how you can release thangs.

Who knew!

Put my life on hold until it gets a little better.

Self-employed just settled with the weather.

New thing full swing old prince to a king.
bloodline offspring watch what I bring.

Move around giants get closer to the tyrants.

Once i do the knowledge I can then apply
science.

Make lazy days off minimum wage there's a
bonus to gain with that extra pay.

Enjoy the funds while working on the run.

At the gates of heaven is not where I'm from.

Whenever kingdom come place hands on a
drum.

Now that's the sound making a mighty joe
young.

Enter the moment like guest who came back.

Twenty-one blackjack comps don't expect
that.

I'm in the cut with new stuff no blind man
bluff.

I'm extraordinary A plus living outside a
cusp.

Cool Destination

Hit the parkway to Philly so I can catch my
flight.
Feeling right within my sight hope the seats
ain't tight.
My dreams of a link chain and a falcon
pendant.
Need a car not rented yet fresh money
scented.
Body fresh smelling from Islamic oils I
dabbed.
Make them fools mad I touch new states and
get cabbed.
Or my peoples push the ride that drop me to
the Telly.
Drop the bags off I am ready singing along to
r Kelly.
Meal and a drink live music and good vibes.
Keep the guard starred like a movie premiere
arrived.
Mixed cultures appear but I don't care it's all
fair.

Feel good, atmosphere no mask it is fresh air.

New inside my old self the galaxy reopened.

Another route chosen on the path I'm exposing.

Word to JWA the archive of king atterberry.

Remain steady if it is heavy, I'm already.

THE "X" AND "KING" factor!

Back in the day it was once spoken that all
should be equal.
Later to find out it really does not exist
amongst the people.
There is still a struggle to fight for freedom,
justice, and equality.
Why shame some people's honesty excuse
you, pardon me?
How can I reach the line of goals while they
play with my soul?
Traveling different paths switching my route
watching the road.
I have dreams from KING for better scenes
living for hope.
Their poisoning our minds speaking of
untested antidotes.
Active inside a practice of view without
consumption.
My obligation is to reconcile a payment of
giving them nothing.
Swim off the island of poverty and come with
prosperity.

Sing songs that free my inner being
capturing melodies.
In this world conditions of confliction
madness of decisions.
Broaden your higher vision
and strengthen your intuition.
Here we are years later modern-day slavery
in this America.
Surrounded by uniformed murderers waiting
while they shake us.
Disguised as the ones who protect there is
no respect.
Through my findings I reject anything that
they project.
Promised land to the poor folks that came
north on a prayer note.
My ancestors before they transitioned left
information through verbal quotes.

Paper wings!

Allow the ink to hit the page I'm already on my way.

Checking for better days there is no time to play.

Surfing upon the wave I am grounded and balanced.

Exploiting my talent, it is apparent how I can manage.

Note pad on deck much respect to my pen game.

Mindset is insane it's hard for me to explain.

Flyer and higher than my conscious on material.

Check whatever is due my new groove is imperial.

King is my name royalty is in my veins.

Move about with Phoenix wings that carry a certain flame.

Internal fire burning the fuel is natural energy.

Cannot destroy my character are you really kidding me.

Resonate with properties captured from outer earth.

Visit another galaxy that showed off my worth.

Transported back through a portal that is formal.

Through my eyes from the sky opened up the ones who saw you.

Word to Lang!

One of the best fresh from out the Skylab on his chest.

Peep the arm tatted crest hear him spit from out the flesh.

Is he a guard of course security stationed on deck?

What you expect I wasn't coming next much due respect.

Champion born inside of Harlem hospital walls.

Make my bars stand tall as if the symphony called.

Use to ride the one train to fifty ninth street in New York.

Transfer to the A hit forty second walk inside the PORT.

In line with others who be waiting for the hound.

Leaving the apple from vacation now I'm headed back in towns.

Demonstrating with obligation to the culture with creation.

I'm too old to be hating or even clout chasing.

Move about in places until I find the right oasis.

Build with certain masons my family been awakened.

Strengthened by higher power energy leave me be.

Don't even to lie to me I only see the truth believed.

Comedian chore when I step through Satan door.

Release my evil sided flaws that's why my camel won't straw.

Released by a force cleansed daily by my faith.

Even my spiritual soulmate won't ever lose her place.

I'm governed by a society of others like myself.

To accept what is written with no problems on my belt.

Inner building!

I ain't even pass dude nor am I past due.

Do whatever I want, yawl trying to be cool.

Trying to change the altitude of flying next to who.

You are not my biological so deuce you and your crew.

If my brother is your brother that is only by a closeness.

Receive this scribe without postage when I post it take notice.

When you speak with my name on your tongue it is a shame.

Support what nigga, of course I am estranged playing a game.

My ideas were my own keep your thoughts in your thoughts.

I am that next level force that is connected to the source.

Do not get lost trying to figure out my steps when i move quick.

My spoken word music have them puzzled
while illusive.

This is Buddhist versus Judas common
sense versus foolish.

Meet the coolest of the coolest one created
by the students.

My time inside the church opened up my
research.

Spiritual earth cleansed the dirt off my pants
also my shirt.

Changed my life for a better cause now I
mastered poetry.

Only one holding me is a trilogy of a brighter
me.

Made my bed where I lay and stay providing
service.

When I make them others nervous it's my
higher calling purpose.

Their greed for a false fed meal off the grain
ticket.

Insulting of how they mimic never will they
ever get it.

Walk this physical plane with my eyes closed
rely on vibes.

It's been one helluva ride getting by with
other eyes.

1,2 1,2 pt.2

Same thing that make you frown can be the
same thing to make you smile.
Different words hitting your spot that you
haven't heard in a while.
Even a preview can be instrumental as if it's
musical.
Allow the vibes to come through you with a
feeling ever so magnificent.
Natural presence so authentic and raised
organic.
From a genuine standard breathing and
sleeping under this planet.
Above my left wrist is a tat of a cross with
red ink.
How about hitting the paper with what we
think and have a drink?
Beverage of choice so refreshing my class is
a glass.
When I'm sitting amongst a team of old
friends from my past.

Rehashing on stories laughing and joking
having big fun.
I love to reminisce, and I don't have to cue a
drummer one!

By all means

My dedication to you women who move
around in different scenes.
Appreciating what you bring by many means
a lot of things.
Strong on the course within your pure
righteous state.
Do your thing I see your face and how you
navigate.
Times be hard while in charge keeping your
day sunny.
Keeping yourself lovely even humorous and
funny.
Grounded by the bases of your heart, mind,
and soul.
Knowing what you know, keeping control
while on the go.
Adapt to environments where the world can
be cold.
Precious women never fold you fight hard to
reach your goal.

Facing challenges of the sexes within
society's checkers.
Working so hard keep in mind where your
point of rest is.
My mother's mother carried the weight
problems on her back.
My fathers' father's mother helped her family
stay on track.
My father's mother's mother stood tall
without crap.
And my mother's father's mother kept family
love intact.

All eyes aside

The way them jeans fit your figure like a
frame holding a picture.
Your signature is the smile that is so
beautiful hear my whispers.
Body so intact forget a compass I need a
map.
I love details to the right female there is no
holding me back.
What is shown that attracted me I know
others watch awkwardly.
If I was a wizard with sorcery, I would blind
sight off of she.
But what I fell in love with I cannot dismiss
god's gift.
Must accept what she is blessed with and
hope she don't get messed with.
I'm a sun sign with a sharp mind that have
plenty of time to enjoy mine.
Finer than grades of wine in a cellar racked
on woods of pine.

So, the only truth to tell is to show that I love freely.

I know longevity isn't easy but I wanna be where you can see me.

Remain the same don't change just respect your mirrored view.

All the things that kept you fresh and new brought me in your cue.

So only question I ask is that you be mindful of the vultures.

There are some in every culture yet baby I support ya.

Father's legacy pt.1

Never tried to be like had my own demons to
fight.
Only outlet was to pick up a pencil and just
write.
What I been through or was into, God have it
charted.
Before my journey got started, I was chillin'
with the sergeant.
I was a lieutenant with loyalty taking trips out
of state.
Man with a different name with my father's
father face.
Cutty G is what they called me hanging with
these street cats.
Did not ever get attacked I was attached to
the pack.
Dude with no emotions just rolling walking a
path.
Same time honing a craft that would get me
where I am at.

But it didn't work out, so I worked out and was content.

Fast like the flash handling task with confidence.

As the years ran by my age moved with my employment.

Even my love and enjoyment doing books started soaring.

The Man behind the hands is a title just for me.

Broke off my mother's leaves and built my father's legacy.

Father's legacy pt.2

So, as I think double sided puppet masters
better watch out.
Before your ass check out or somebody take
your clock out.
Some kill me with that opportunist mentality I
rather be.
Conserving my energy around those that be
feeling me.
Building towers of humility for jokers acting
silly.
Them complexes of bad ass Billy's will die
quickly.
Streets have no love for manipulators who
pound and hug.
I am what the real brothers once was, we in
the cut.
Pops taught me a few things that I never ever
talk about.
So, when I am out and about I keep that
energy in not out.

So, my soul is never compromised by
misguided spirits.
Understand these lyrics if you can and get
near it.
What I did not know before is exactly what
I've learned.
How many times can you get burned by a
society with no lamps.
Too much shade displayed, is the world a big
arcade.
Found my niche inside a page showing me
the KINGS WAVE!

CONSIDERATE FEELINGS

Masquerade of affection

Walk inside the highest form of heartfelt
devotion.
Where the cards are on the table and life is in
motion.
Once again, it's the happening that is
occurring inside.
Feeling revived I survived saying goodbye to
what died.
No longer bittersweet nor any high
expectations.
My spirit free from slowly waiting on time I
have been patient.
Walk into the joy of knowing great moments
can still exist.
Giving your love the greatest kiss as I walk
out from the mist.
Make plans without demand as we travel into
what's new.
Play around with somethings ideas are out
the blue.
Set up ways for more enjoyable, pleasurable
sentiments.

Been loving you ever since let's take what ifs off the fence.

Prepare the next level of excitement to your daily routine.

Provide gifts that don't exist on your wish list I have deemed.

Share a table of confidence made of tender, love and care.

Just be aware of how sincere I would like to inhale your air.

Hold my thoughts within your world of knowing what's being shown.

I'm building a strong foundation that is condoned with this poem.

Let's be together as one believe me you are not alone.

Touch the interest of your internal soul welcome me home.

Get next to

If I forgot there's a hidden message out the box.

Recorded just for you now playing is something hot.

They thought that I was done my return is coming soon.

Sun is shining bright healing all your wounds.

Hands hold power conversation on your physical.

Open the door shoot my shot to you.

Plan to be a winner I am good member.

Fly inside the season of spring from out winter.

Guided by a purpose of life I just might.

Relax before midnight with a nice delight.

Playing surface through my Bluetooth speakers.

Don't ask about my date I was glad to meet her.

After have you seen her there's nothing that's between us.

Two adults waiting on God to roll fever.
My steps are taken with patience love is
vacant.
Start off as friends start dating to love
making.
Could it be trial or error maybe a nice
pleasure?
General experience is to serve kind gesture.

My goodness

She wants a pleasure principle who can work
nontraditional.
Allow her body to form melody and rhythms
internally.
Become the highlight of a kissing bandit that
is heard so much about.
Enjoying a course upon a route being
witnessed inside her house.
Airwaves controlled by a connective
impulsive energy.
Sounds bringing memories that was lost for
centuries.
Modern day emotions and feelings from a
touch and smiling stare.
Undressing each other's wears until flesh
moment appear.
Romantically dancing, intimacy covers this
one night.
Her ticket on the JWA flight is exactly right.
Bedroom misty from marijuana being
exhaled.

As we lay thinking about all the past times
that failed.
Due to the power of NOW we are
experiencing the happening.
One for trouble two time we get to know each
other practicing.

Uncharted territory

Beautiful moments with cashmere
conversations.
Whether we are seeing each other or simply
dating.
Clock the challenges of space before the
hours fold.
Allow a story untold building up a higher
goal.
My spirit raises certain vibrations free to you.
Open doors unexplored with a vernacular
view.
All seem fine on point without a clue.
How about we do what we do while it's fresh
and brand new.
Smell of fresh fruit your fragrance is
appetizing.
As our eyes match each other with the
temperature rising.
Hand's touch, sensual kiss with no direction.
Points of affection is righteous what a
blessing.
No expectation on the chill but feel the thrill.

A lot of time to kill without falling downhill.

Stamp of approval what's next is nothing less.

She found the poet Joel Washington Atterbury at his best.

As I recite words of pleasure absorbing the energy she displays.

Told her this poem is from me to you pt.2 king's wave.

Time before

Use to dream that I mastered many ways to capture.

Covered your whole rapture moved in a little faster.

Could not fall short on the steps to get to know you.

Speaking to you on the phone felt very soulful.

Conversation and laughter about so many things.

Schedule a time to meet up and see how we can swing.

Perhaps lunch or dinner your choice I do not mind.

What was sought and kept divine I placed in these lines.

Your glow so incredible that the angels get jealous.

It's just another side of gods glorious creation that he treasures.

There is no need to wonder if we make it to the summer.
It is you and I no extra numbers because I'm not a runner.

Only you

Special notice to your door presentation to your heart.

Lift the veil and just inhale my gentle cycle when I start.

Hold your hands rubbing the center of your palms remain calm.

Absorb the sound that's real warm listening to these songs.

Let the music play as we speak within each other.

Kissing the aura which is a beautiful color before supper.

Nice meal displayed with glasses of wine filled.

It's not about a sealed deal I'm the wind on the mill.

Plenty of time to kill with a diamond back skill.

Touch the surface of your needs as we relax and chill.

Enjoy the session which is a blessing of joy to the night.

Keep a dimness to the lights as I recite what I write.

All natural to capture you with something new.

Keep in mind what we can do after we check points of view.

My visual and mental create waves of vibes sensual.

This is part two from a new book kings' wave from me to you.

LANGUAGE TO MANAGE pt.1

She like to touch my hands after days of
missing me.
Believing In all that she sees without judging
me.
When I show up the mask is down giving a
kiss.
Expressing how much she miss way back
she knew prince.
Lord atterberry who was waiting to be
revived.
Didn't receive the lifeline until I started
raising vibes.
Love seen love shown I just go with the flow.
Respect all that's in her soul because of how
I have grown.
If I'm trash to the women who don't like what
I represent.
I am treasured by the women who have
magnificent confidence.

Age does not matter it's the heart mind and soul.
Share my pieces just like recesses and that's how king roll.

Triangle angle

It's been thirty days since you been on my
mind.
Another thirty wondering if I should seek and
find.
But if all is going well perhaps, I'm yours and
your mine.
That's an early thirty worthy manifesting
some great time.
Converse unrehearsed with good intention
just to see.
If everything is cool and we are sharing some
great chemistry.
Consideration on the table and strong
possible vibes.
Nobody want to be hurt with them lies that
are disguised.
So, my verbal letter words fair exchange
towards us creating.
Building off high anticipation while every
week communicating.

The decision to continue is in review because it's new.

This is the shot that I shoot I think this time it's due.

Let me know if I can feed you with that love that you deserve.

Are you a customer of trust here are some well-spoken words?

Feeling good deep inside did I arrive with no goodbyes.

Thirty degrees on 3 points within a 90-day demise.

Kiss from a rose

Only during the moonlight, I feel your
emotions deep inside of me.
Wherever your thoughts may be let me send
you what your eyes cannot see.
May this letter of sentiment address anything
you hope for.
Allow my drive and motivation to open a
window or a door.
If I may enter only to bring you with me on a
nice peaceful journey.
You will never worry travel early to a place
where love is worthy.
The skies are an exceptional light as the sun
beam through clouds of joy.
Filling each other's void as we embrace each
other's choice.
Memorizing one another's expression so we
can hold dear to heart.
Start with a kiss that will spark something
magical as we mark.

The moment that begins and extend to a beautiful win.

Placing the flowers upon showers of words that represent.

Only reason that I accept what you bring is just because.

Of a feeling inside us we can trust and never discuss.

Lose control while we take in the time that we have here.

It's the kiss from a rose that appear when love is near.

It's on the spot

This is a letter to my lady friend hello here
you are.
A different side of king that can open your
body parts.
Place you in a mood that make your body
move.
No need for music my vibes provide the
groove.
My fingers touch your flesh like a pianist on a
keyboard.
The portal to explore in your hall is an allure.
Testing all the notes until I find a certain
sound.
Might go downtown till your mind is out of
bounds.
Place you on my lap as I touch that pussy
cat.
Rubbing your neck and back just relax and
climax.
Slow flow attack through a past life
attraction.

Sending you back in time so you remember what is happening.
The feel is real no over drill inside your well.
As I hump and pump until I hear your silent wail.
Kiss all concerns away we on our way.
Fantastic voyage out the sheets we sideways.
Your thighs so nice and thick I'm loving your hips.
Exhibit no limits we good until we finished.
Rock me with toppy until your mouth gets sloppy.
Wax on and wax off baby I'm your Miyagi.

Open window pt.2

My conversation ain't the same since I met you.
Vibrating at a frequency that I wanna get next to.
Thinking to myself on my days of stillness.
Hope the words in this poem can help you feel this.
Allow my adequate time to show another part of me.
With the power of my poetry shower, you with energy.
Thoughts from my paper verbalized through music.
Peep this exclusive showing amusing usage.
Put me up in high regard while you seek and find.
Don't worry about the signs my life path is nine.
Signature already in place no need to check.
I do what I do on any level of respect.

Let me know if this is what you want or need.
While my spirit is free just keep it real me.
Make a full promise to be honest and cool.
A lot of things I am into are essential with
potential.

22 with you

I'm walking another course without your
memory in my thoughts.
It was your loss when you were caught did
you forget what you were taught.
Maybe your mom's teachings wasn't mindful
to your heart.
I'm like ughh stop reminding me what you
lost we been apart.
Now you show up at the door and explore
what could I need.
What's in the bag aww come on my favorite
food to eat.
And some minced apple pie with some henny
on the side.
Damn I cannot hide the intimate notion you
apply.
Sweet words and kind gestures shit getting
me messed up.
What the fuck? Oh, well may as well push all
my luck.

Finding myself watching a movie sitting with you on the couch.

Hugging and kissing, dear lord, what is this shit all about?

Apologetic conversations about our offset situations.

We both was really wasting a lot of patience where the days went.

Ugly moods destructive now rebuilt on newer structures.

Admitting how much we love us and returning as lovers.

King!

Leave it Alone

Guess I'm not the type yet still another feel.
Keeping me in her heart through expression
revealed.
Showing me what a woman can see inside of
me.
Knowing exactly how to be when she
releases her energy.
Supportive when I'm down never worried
about my frown.
Kissing my days with a smile feeling like I'm
in a lounge.
Sound of music atmosphere I'm the only
she's near.
Not kept inside the rear placed away like
souvenirs.
On front street between look and listen
boulevard.
One thing she asked from the start is respect
her heart.
Unhidden is me not a possibility or thought.
I'm the one she sees unlike before to adore.

ELEVATED MAINFRAME

In mind I'm mental

Some never appreciated what I brought to
the table.
I ain't feel the cheap shots so I release from
the navel.
Power source high from the house of the
creator.
I be enjoying all the haters with they bullshit
capers.
Sand slip from your hand while you throw
rocks and laugh.
Been seen your trash I'm not impressed
when you brag.
Only time I ever see you is when your acting
the fool.
When I drop a few jewels knowledge return
from out the blue.
Everything is cool I see the world as a circus.
What happened to the purpose of service too
many nervous.
Walk into division of living without
restrictions.

Speaking to many women I'm friendly in my position.
Single and available the draft is coming soon.
Better scoop the king up before I become a groom.
Life can be exciting when invited to share some big fun.
One honey cooking chicken beans and rice calling me handsome.
I'm not even a player just a gentleman wishing I'm better than.
The average who gained status what matters is how we begin.
Let us begin I'm Washington mixed with Atterbury's.
My story is glory I beat the odds on secondary.
New glow new hope new dope and official.
It's was only a matter of time before my world kiss you.

Enjoyment

Some days are better than others Some days
are a mystery.
Without judgement clouding my train of
thought I take a ride to the beach in cape
May.
Skies are bright sunshine exposing its
beautiful rays upon the people.
As I walk across the sand feeling the
radiance of a clearance coming upon me.
No second guessing about the day I am
about to endure.
Watching the waves in the water touch land
of sand and wonder.
Just how peaceful this setting is, many years
ago I didn't appreciate.
Nowadays I meditate and pray searching for
heavens lovely gates.
What a delight upon sight as I am watching
many cultures in their chairs.
Accommodation is welcomed by the creator
who controls all that exist.

Birds flying high and low as their flight
patterns are shown.
Aww man what a nice way to grow a smile
inside the physical body.
I know everything isn't for everybody, but
KING adore the natural occurrences.
So as the weight of the world and its issues
are lifted, I can enjoy an afternoon while
handling my business.

Dreams of dreams!

What was will never be what is can become destiny.

Move around naturally inside a place of odyssey.

Ignite a flame of what you desire breathe air on what expired.

If what admired can be salvaged utilizing gods wire.

Memo taken on the wake up improvise on uncertainty.

Address what is lately through colors navy blue, gold and burgundy.

Embody feelings from where you were that raise your existence.

Come close to what is distant so there's no longer distance.

Behind the front beyond the present absorb interjected lessons.

Mind over matter find a master blaster opening doors to question.

Solution to equation fraction of realness
inside the eyes closed.

Sensory telling the untold in-which unfold on
written scrolls.

For the world who knew!

Tackle topics in society for the shadow
people hiding out.
Trouble in they house issues around nobody
know about.
Smiles created in fun times frowning when
somebody home.
Emotional cyclones ending a cycle of love
unknown.
What use to be easy to live inside of a
comforter.
Lost the light source to a darkness that
manifested a monster.
Convo to a penner or a ear receiving lender.
Air was once thinner becoming thick losers
and winners.
Content weak on the speech drawing heat.
False elaboration drawing a disappointed
greet.
Silence golden why keep holding on what's
dozing.

Stop loading on legs strolling they not the one chosen.

Notice to the facts that's formed inside alarms.

Don't get marveled by the charm might be a mental bomb.

With or without a timer peep the liners of the margin.

In life may have to pardon but excuse the tools bargained.

IT'S THE KING

Thinking back to a time around nineteen
ninety-one.
Found knowledge of self and my new life
begun.
Chose to be better than the other side of me.
Studied under the gods and earths building
degrees.
My spirit never compromised what I felt in
heart.
Learned to formulate my words and spit
darts.
Traveled to certain boroughs before I miss
curfew.
Disciplinarians would hurt you about circles.
Lessons learned in life understanding right
and wrong.
Nowadays I perform poems and bang them
into songs.
Go outside the norm my sequence of
enlightenment.

Senses so heightened I do not need to have requirements.

Traveling through time

If I went there from out of nowhere who would really care.

Allow myself to prepare and be aware of what others share.

Memories in her diaries and the pages from my journal.

Found inside a place that don't concern you the disloyal.

All that my eyes see inside what is meant for us.

Transportation provided no need for trains or a bus.

Location locked in present presence heartly coded.

Everything else truly noted therefor path is chosen.

Lonely motives of the seeker give the reader and believers.

Findings of the dreamer's, teachers, speakers I'm a man with fathered features. Walk into another day, visit all the house that pray.

Searching for some better ways, can't embrace what nayers say.

Traveling through time connect directly to the divine.

Hope and faith give you a piece of mind let go of past timelines.

Pray on interventions if society doesn't listen.

Focus on your mission with vision and keep living.

Simplistic richness

All I ever wanted was something better and
different.
Special with nice interest refusing to live on
ignorance.
Motivation of giving, receiving the greatest
blessing.
Articulate conversation addressing the
smallest questions.
Never thinking to low stay grounded below
the high.
Middle session on the rise untying ribbons
from the sky.
Don't judge the buzz that's created to level
us.
At the end of the day painting a picture
without a brush.
The rush left in the dust walk in the sun.
Raised up as one put in that work came from
the slums.
Build projects off plans on diagrams and
programs.

Become my Wonder Woman I'm just enjoying being a fan.

As a man loving a strong beautiful presence around me.

Dating your heart if your mind free this is K.I.N.G.

Gentleman with a hand that's been known to hold it down.

Two feet on the ground standing firm wearing a crown.

Rock it tilted to the left because I know what feels right.

Excuse me baby we gonna be alright let's take flight.

Closure

All chapters closed before I didn't know.

It wasn't written on the wall and painted on a window.

Sight of vision blurred to what really occurred.

Did I get what I deserved maybe her life was lost in words.

Lines of truth unspoken action seen from vivid dreams.

Was it a nightmare from light years dirtied from being clean?

My eyes only accept what shine early from my birth.

Third eye from outer earth helped me to avoid being hurt.

Progress after the process about nonsense I had left.

Built a armor so I am calmer than a marriage that felt death.

Kept peace inside the beautiful side of me and just continue.

Living my life without the preview and remain with gods' people.

The sequel of never wanting to see or hear from you.

There is a time and place for everything with others that bend you.

The memory of a misery so dark ugly and fucked up.

Heard you wanna contact me I'm living right now so what!

Forever Love

When she left, I couldn't imagine being
focused on my goals.
So, when opportunity came about I set high
for the road.
She reminded me of a struggle to survive
between love and hurt.
Opening to me upbeat yet feeling down on
her worse.
Knowing she won't be around long enough to
see me rise.
Only time could really tell when she would
face her demise.
With that strain on my thoughts, I walked in
between many scenes.
I loved her so much started having broken
dreams.
Searching for answers how could she leave
me alone.
I guess the better living place was her new
beautiful home.
Didn't feel right to me but to leave was her
response.

For months, my mother knew she wouldn't
be around for me long.
Now that I am grown, and these memories
appear.
She is the best woman I ever got know loving
that shared.

The love in you

Since we been together all that's shown will continue.
Even if times get tough view my demeanor menu.
Serving plates of loyalty and a side dish of honesty.
My modesty solidifies my warm heart warranty.
You're the one that I wake up to in the morning like breakfast.
After the time moves forward bearing witness to freshness.
Before I close my lids kiss your thoughts before I sleep.
It's these pleasurable measures that keep me loving you queen.
You make me feel so good with all the things that you do.
Even surprising my spirit when it's outside of you.

Holding on to what we have in advance just in case.

We ever lose faith and our bond start to break.

Comfort your feelings of emotion whichever way they flow.

Reintroduce myself to your soul from a long time ago.

Looking inside your eyes as if the first time we met.

Remembering your sweet-smelling breath and the nice skin flesh.

I can't see myself with wandering eyes or inappropriate conversations.

Only you can make me happy just like our few months of dating.

There's nothing new that I want or slip and fall into another.

You're my everything and more baby let's keep other covered.

Moment of memory

Guided by the radiance of her spirit she
brought me into her world.
Fascinated by the outside place she read my
aqua thoughts.
Walking through the park as we moved
across grass onto a path.
Sat next to each other on the rocks watching
the water collide.
Sun shining bright energizing our inner life.
This magnificent setting is a wonderful
delight.
One of many locations reminding me of my
own sacred place.
As the ray beam from the sky strike lightly
upon our face.
During our conversation enjoying company
of her and I.
With elevated vibes creating energetic
expression from our eyes.
Smiling and laughing joking and kidding
around.

Without sounds of music this kind gesture is found.

So, what I recall is the profound beauty I observed.

Special moments like this can have you lost for words.

No doubt!

My mind take flight hit heights shine bright.
Even at night feel right with my third sight.
So many lost worrying about other problems.
Dodge them can't solve them self-healing
have to mark them.
Take righteous steps to resurrect what's
hurting you.
Perhaps pray and meditate maybe that will
rescue.
All the in between that's been absorbed in
your physical.
Watch what's next to you if it doesn't feel
true.
Love what is, never what's supposed to be.
Get caught in an aura of total disbelief.
See inside the world of past troubles and
issues.
For some time, I heard whistles that showed
what others been through.
No real alarm to warn catch a song.

Sing and rejoice therefore your heart can get strong.
Understand your worth even if you're feeling down.
There's a higher purpose to life don't allow yourself to drown.

This live video show which is displayed on Facebook Live and YouTube is hosted by myself, KING ATTERBERRY and produced by my cousin Quinten Ford on the amazing the Let's Talk platform.

We invite spoken word artists from around the nation to appear and recite their material on this virtual platform.

So please come check the show out!

If you are interested to appear on the show, feel free to email me and pass the word!

Joel Washington Atterberry

AUTHOR / POET & CREATIVE WRITER

❖

KING ATTERBERRY INK

(609) 408-3396

IG: mentallity9 / king_atterberry7 | kingatterberry7@gmail.com
Facebook: JOEL WASHINGTON
ATTERBERRY

Scan QR CODE FOR INFO